Baby Mammals

Bobbie Kalman
Crabtree Publishing Company
www.crabtreebooks.com

It's fun to learn about Baby Animals

Created by Bobbie Kalman

Dedicated to Carter and Madison Girotti

With much love from

Auntie Kat and Uncle Matt

**Author and
Editor-in-Chief**
Bobbie Kalman

Editors
Kathy Middleton
Crystal Sikkens

Photo research
Bobbie Kalman

Design
Bobbie Kalman
Katherine Berti
Samantha Crabtree
(logo and front cover)

Print and production coordinator
Katherine Berti

Prepress technician
Katherine Berti

Illustrations
Bonna Rouse: pages 8, 24 (skeleton and lungs)

Photographs
Corel: page 11 (top left)
Digital Vision: page 13 (top left)
Dreamstime: page 11 (middle left)
All other images by Shutterstock

Library and Archives Canada Cataloguing in Publication

Kalman, Bobbie
    Baby mammals / Bobbie Kalman.

(It's fun to learn about baby animals)
Includes index.
Issued also in electronic formats.
ISBN 978-0-7787-1008-0 (bound).--ISBN 978-0-7787-1013-4 (pbk.)

    1. Mammals--Infancy--Juvenile literature. I. Title. II. Series:
It's fun to learn about baby animals

QL706.2.K347 2013   j599.13'92   C2012-907318-0

Library of Congress Cataloging-in-Publication Data

CIP available at Library of Congress

Crabtree Publishing Company
www.crabtreebooks.com   1-800-387-7650

Published in Canada
Crabtree Publishing
616 Welland Ave.
St. Catharines, Ontario
L2M 5V6

Published in the United States
Crabtree Publishing
PMB 59051
350 Fifth Avenue, 59th Floor
New York, New York 10118

Published in the United Kingdom
Crabtree Publishing
Maritime House
Basin Road North, Hove
BN41 1WR

Published in Australia
Crabtree Publishing
3 Charles Street
Coburg North
VIC, 3058

Printed in Hong Kong/012013/BK20121102

What is in this book?

What is a mammal?

Mammals are animals that have hair or fur on their bodies. Mammals grow inside the bodies of their mothers and are **born**. Some mammal mothers give birth to one or two babies, and others, like rats, have many babies.

Taking care

Most mammal mothers take good care of their babies. They teach them how to find food and stay safe.

These lambs were just born. Their mother licks them clean.

Baby giraffes stay with their mothers for almost two years before they live on their own.

Drinking mother's milk

Mammal mothers make milk in their bodies to feed

their babies. Drinking mother's milk is called **nursing**.

Mammal babies nurse soon after they are born. As the

babies grow, they nurse less often and start eating the

same foods as their parents. Some mammal mothers,

like dogs, nurse several babies at the same time.

Kinds of mammals

There are different kinds of mammals.
Each mammal belongs to a group. Some
mammal groups are shown on these pages.
How many kinds of mammals do you know?

*Monkeys, apes, lemurs,
and people are* **primates**
(see pages 20–21).

*Squirrels
are* **rodents**
(see page 16).

*The kitten and
lion cub both belong
to the* **carnivora**
group (see page 19).

*Some mammals, like horses,
have* **hoofs** *(see page 14).*

Bats are mammals that can fly (see page 22).

A baby kangaroo lives and grows inside its mother's pouch (see page 18).

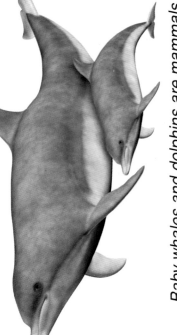

Baby whales and dolphins are mammals that live in oceans (see page 23).

Elephants make up their own group of mammals (see page 15).

Rabbits and hares belong to another group of mammals (see page 17).

Baby sloths spend most of their lives in trees (see page 22).

Mammal bodies

A mammal has a group of bones, called a **backbone**, in the middle of its back. Animals that have backbones are called **vertebrates**. Mammals also have **limbs**. A limb can be an arm, leg, flipper, or wing. Mammals use their limbs to walk, run, climb, swim, or fly.

All the bones in an animal's body make up its **skeleton**. The skeleton on the left is a monkey's skeleton.

This monkey has four limbs. Its limbs are legs. People have two arms and two legs.

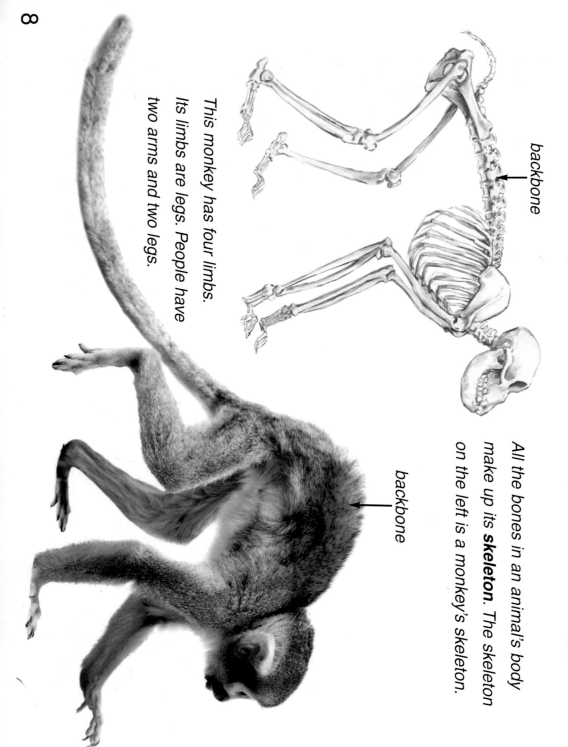

backbone

backbone

Warm blood

Mammals are **warm-blooded**. The body temperature of warm-blooded animals stays about the same in both warm and cold weather. Some mammals have thick fur coats that keep them warm in cold weather. Mammals that live in warm climates have less fur or hair.

This polar bear **cub**, or baby, has a thick layer of **blubber**, or fat, under its skin. It also has two layers of warm fur.

Breathing air

Mammals have **lungs** for breathing air. Lungs are inside their bodies. They take in air and let out air. Mammals that live in water must swim to the surface to breathe. Dolphins, whales, and seals live in water. They breathe air above water.

Homes of baby mammals

Mammals live all over the world in many kinds of **habitats**. A habitat is a natural place where an animal lives. Most mammals live in land habitats, such as forests, mountains, grasslands, and deserts, but some live in water habitats. Oceans, rivers, and lakes are water habitats.

These goat babies, called kids, live high on mountains.

Baby chipmunks live in forests and other habitats with trees. They sleep in underground **burrows**, or holes.

Kit foxes live in dry areas called **deserts**. Their big ears let heat out of their bodies.

This mule deer mother and **fawn** live in a **prairie**, or grassy area with few trees.

Many apes and monkeys live in forests in warm areas of Earth. This mother and baby orangutan live high in trees.

Polar bears live in the Arctic, a cold area in the northern part of Earth.

Whales, dolphins, seals, and some other mammals live in oceans.

Mothers and babies

Baby mammals are helpless when they are born. They need their mothers to feed them and keep them safe. How do baby mammals learn to **survive**, or stay alive? Animals cannot learn all the things that you can, but they do need to learn important things to survive. Their mothers teach them how to communicate, find food, move around their habitats, and stay safe.

Red fox mothers teach their kits to find mice and rabbits to eat. Foxes are **predators**. They hunt other animals.

Baby mammals communicate using sounds and **gestures**, or movements. This baby orangutan is "talking" to her mother. Her mother listens with love.

Elephant calves need their mothers and other elephant mothers to care for them and teach them how to find food and water. They cannot survive on their own.

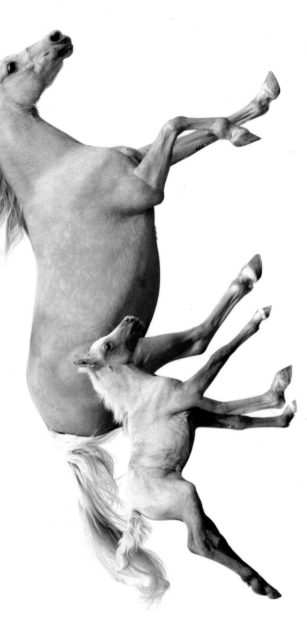

Mammals move in different ways. They swim, walk, run, and climb. Some even fly. **Foals**, or baby horses, walk shortly after they are born. They soon start running with their mothers.

Babies with hoofs

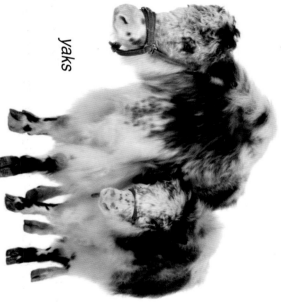

Mammals with hoofs are called **ungulates**. Hoofs protect the feet of these animals and help them move. Some mammals climb, and some walk and run. Zebras and horses have a single hoof on each foot. Sheep, goats, and giraffes have two-toed hoofs, and rhinoceroses have hoofs with three parts.

The hoofs of bighorn lambs and yaks have two toes, or parts. The toes can split to help the animals grip rocks as they climb. Two toes help keep the animals from slipping while they climb high mountains.

The hoofs of zebras and horses have one part.

bighorn lamb

yaks

Rhinoceroses have three-toed hoofs.

Elephant calves

Elephants are the biggest land mammals. There are three kinds of elephants. They are Asian elephants, African forest elephants, and African savanna elephants. Elephant babies are called **calves**. Elephants have long trunks. They use their trunks for lifting and exploring.

Asian elephants have small ears and two bumps on their heads. Very few have **tusks**. *Tusks are long pointed teeth.*

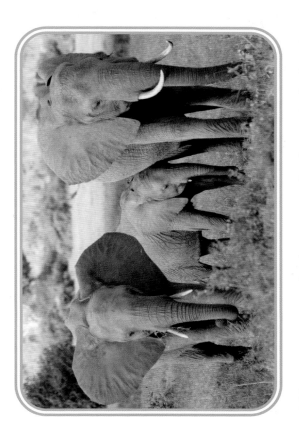

African savanna elephants are the largest elephants. They have huge ears and curved tusks.

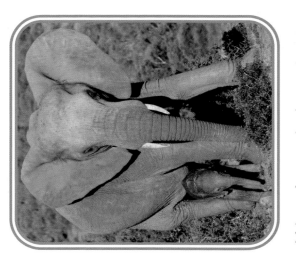

African forest elephants have straight tusks and rounded ears.

Rodent babies

Rodents are mammals with four long, sharp, front teeth. The teeth never stop growing. Rodents chew on hard things to keep their teeth sharp and to wear them down so they will not grow too long. Many rodents are born blind and without hair.

rats

Mice and rats are rodents that can be found almost everywhere! Mothers give birth to many babies at one time. The babies are blind and have no fur.

Baby squirrels are called kits or pups.

Chipmunks are born underground. They find food above ground and in trees.

Baby porcupines are born with soft **quills**, or spines. Their eyes are closed at birth.

Rabbits, hares, and pikas

Rabbits also have long front teeth that keep growing, but they are not rodents. They are mammals called **lagomorphs**. Hares and pikas also belong to this group of mammals. All these animals are **herbivores**. Herbivores eat only plants.

Bunnies, or baby rabbits, are born blind and hairless.

Mother rabbits feed and care for their bunnies for about two months.

Leverets, or baby hares, are covered in fur and can see when they are born. Their mother does not take care of them for very long.

Pikas have small rounded ears and short tails. They live in rocky areas. Baby pikas are called **pikettes**.

Marsupial joeys

Most mammal babies are fully developed before they are born, but **marsupial** babies, called **joeys**, are tiny and can not live without their mothers.

Most marsupial mothers have a **pouch**, or pocket, in which the babies continue to grow after they are born. They live and nurse in the pouch for weeks or months before they are ready to come out. Kangaroos, koalas, and opossums are marsupials.

After a young koala joey comes out of the pouch, it clings to its mother's chest. An older joey rides on its mother's back.

A kangaroo joey does not leave its mother's pouch for six to eight months. It then starts leaving for a few minutes at a time. At about nine months, the joey leaves the pouch for good.

opossums

Sharp teeth

Mammals with sharp teeth and long, pointed claws belong to the carnivora group. Some of the mammals in this group are **carnivores**, or animals that eat other animals. Others that belong to the carnivora group are **omnivores**. Omnivores eat both plants and meat.

This polar bear cub is a carnivore, but other bears eat plants as well as other animals.

Raccoons belong to the carnivora group, but they eat plants, too.

All cats, like this lion cub, are carnivores. They have four long, pointed teeth that are sharp for tearing meat. These special teeth are called **canine** *teeth.*

Foxes have sharp teeth and claws. They hunt and eat other animals, but they also eat plants.

Smart primates

Primates are the smartest animals. They have big brains, which allow them to learn many things. Monkeys, apes, lemurs, and humans are primates. Gorillas are big primates. Gorillas are big primates, but some primates, such as bush babies, are very small.

Gorillas are the biggest primates. They are animals called apes.

Ring-tailed lemurs live in Africa.

Bush babies are small primates that live in Africa.

Monkeys are smaller than apes. They have tails.

This boy uses his fingers and thumbs to type on a laptop. His big brain allows him to learn many things. Humans are the smartest primates.

Primate mothers, like the ruffed lemur above, take good care of their babies. Many lemurs and other primates live in big groups.

Fingers and thumbs

Most primates have hands with fingers and **opposable** thumbs. An opposable thumb can touch the opposite fingers of the same hand. It allows primates to hold objects, such as tools, easily.

This chimpanzee is using his opposable thumb to grab a stick. He uses the stick as a tool to get food.

Other mammals

You have seen several mammal groups in this book, but there are many more! Sloths, whales and dolphins, manatees, bats, anteaters, and platypuses belong to other mammal groups. Learn more about these interesting animals on these pages.

Bats are mammals that fly. They are not birds because they have no feathers. The biggest bats are called flying foxes. This flying fox mother is nursing her baby.

two-toed sloth

The young sloth above and the tamandua mother and baby below belong to the same animal group. These animals live in South American forests. The tamandua also lives in grassy areas near water.

tamandua

Platypuses live in Australia. They look like a cross between a beaver and a duck. Most mammal babies are born, but baby platypuses **hatch**, or come out of eggs. The babies are called **puggles**.

Manatees are also known as sea cows. Their babies are called calves. Manatees live in warm oceans and in slow-moving rivers that are near oceans. This manatee calf is nursing, but it will eat plants that grow in water when it gets older. Manatees are herbivores.

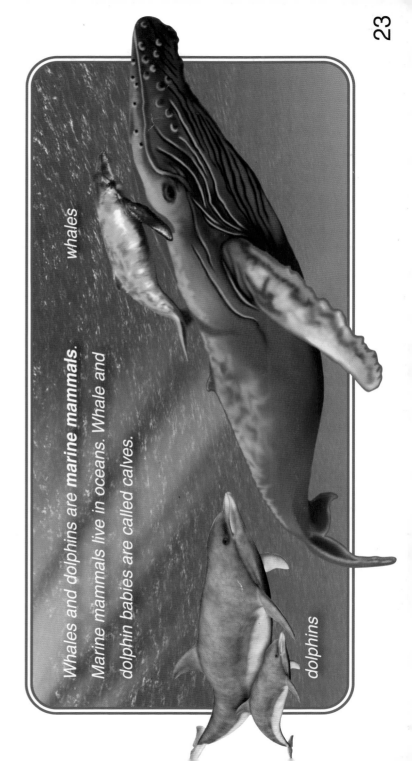

whales

Whales and dolphins are **marine mammals**. Marine mammals live in oceans. Whale and dolphin babies are called calves.

dolphins

Words to know and Index

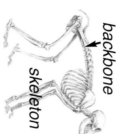

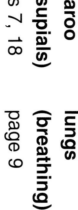

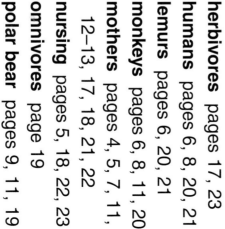

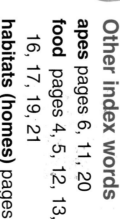